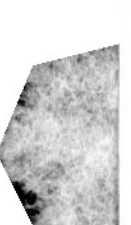

I0792030

Father and Son

Poetry from the Soul

LARRY DICKENS

authorHOUSE

AuthorHouse™ UK
1663 Liberty Drive
Bloomington, IN 47403 USA
www.authorhouse.co.uk
Phone: UK TFN: 0800 0148641 (Toll Free inside the UK)
        UK Local: (02) 0369 56322 (+44 20 3695 6322 from outside the UK)

Published by AuthorHouse 11/10/2022

ISBN: 978-1-6655-9636-7 (sc)
ISBN: 978-1-6655-9635-0 (e)

I wrote this book over many years, dedicated to my son Zach who is and will always be asking questions.

Writing poetry was never meant to be anything other than an outward expression of all the inner turmoil and joyful things that has engulfed me over 40 years, this collection doesn't have a definitive theme, it is simple as it is, raw, awkward in its structure, at times unable to find sense in a senseless world, but it has texture, its tapestry is woven not by clever words but with real experiences. I began writing after being inspired by Edgar Allen Poe, you may find similar themes in Two Black Feathers, A Black Raven and Cracked.

Yet it is not all darkly lit, there is lightness too, such as My Son Zach who is the very reason for this book, another poem well worth reading is Pimley Bridge, a nostalgic trip along the old canal of Pimley when boys were boys and girls knotted Daisies in endless meadow fields.

Poetry is a search for some inner self, to investigate what it is that makes for who we all are, it raises as many questions as it does provide answers, it is in essence the souls voice to words we cannot find ourselves.

To enjoy this book, read it with the care, treat it gently like you might handle a butterfly, read it slowly so that the words don't just fall in, but rather read it as if you have an eternity. As an example of expressing this, most people enjoy karaoke, and love to sing their favourite songs, but some people sing and ruin a song and remain oblivious to being tone deaf, therefore, tread lightly as the best poetry can be delivered awfully if not read with a pace that is deserving of its narrative.

The poetry is a real reflection of my life, the ups and the downs, central to everything is love, it is a journey that takes you on a rollercoaster ride of emotions, just as you think it settles along comes another poem that rips away at the heart.

What if, is a poem that was inspired as with many it was about a changing point of view, love, life and marriage is far more than chemistry, it is deeper, meaningful filled with purpose, a journey of self-discovery.

Vampires was a nightmare born out of sleep deprivation, it follows hot on the heels of Sleep Paralysis, both are events that were lived out, both were frequent night-time companions whether wanted or not.

As a Christian there are many references of my life journey in faith, it is not that this is a collection of poems based upon walking in faith, rather it is told as Christ in me, and how we as human beings stare beyond the stars with wonder when that wonder has been with us from the beginning.

 LARRY DICKENS

Contents

My Son Zach

Written on the birth of my son who will always light up my world.

Your platinum locks
Were heaven sent
A perfect smile
To hearts content

To hold you near
With bright blue eyes
Your tender kisses
And gentle sighs

Your tiny steps
My God did bless
Those tiny feet
That do impress

Just like the moon
And all the stars
They shine a light
Just like you do

Your joyful face
As you spy a rook
When you read
Your Gruffalo books

There's no compare
When we hear you sing?
The love you bring
Is the love we share.

 LARRY DICKENS

Snowekkling

As the storms outside blew in fiercely with snow inside we
watched with awe

Christmas time is once again
There's magic in the air
Whispers travel with the sound of bells, jingling
Oh, what great expectations to be had

Children wrapped up in their beds
Under a canvas filled with stars
Presents wrapped under the tree
All sizes shapes and colours too

Snowekkling fierce outside a blizzard
A winters night true
A story told as events unfold
A story just for you

What if?

What if we held each other's hands?
Closer each day and never make plans
What if we walked in the rain?
And gathered up tears and never complain

So, what if we never make love again
Do we not share the same grain?
The physical elements that make up me
Are made from God who makes up you

What if all we have is each other?
Is it not enough and more than we deserve?
For we both have God who is our mother
Our father our sister and brother

What if all I do is kiss your lips
Do you not also kiss mine?
And does it not taste sweeter than wine
Even with the passing of time

What if you don't see me in a while
Because the places between us runs for miles
Does not your heart still beat for me
Does God our father not set us free

   LARRY DICKENS

My love my joy my peace inside
What if we had never met
In God we would confide
And do you think he would forget

What if all we have is hope
Does not our hope belong in Jesus
Who came with love as he spoke?
With words did he not free us

What if a thousand years passed
Would I forget you or you me?
Does God not save the best till last?
As we pray on bended knee

What if my love it all seems far away?
And every plan we have is not our own
Does God not count every second of each day?
And make His will to us well known

What if we just say thank you Lord
And praise His name above the earth
Does not our father give us reward
For he called us long before our birth.

Prescriptive Love

Could be blond or brunette
Eyes blue brown or green
Might be slim, overweight or curvy
Young, old, black or white
She might like pasta bake or rice
She could be smart and very clever
Or hellhound into leather
She may stare beyond the window
And compare me to the snow
Or she may simply dream of love
And a knight from God above
She may prefer a peaceful life
And become a loving wife
Or she could simply be
The girl I want for me

 LARRY DICKENS

Blind Bends

Blind bends ahead
Turning in too late
I never saw it coming
From the very first date

Her perfume intoxicating
Losing control
I offered her a ring
Now I'm paying the toll

She dressed herself up
Before dressing me down
Those sexy half cups
Were the envy of the town

Driven with desire
I'd race her to the wire
Where I caught a left hook
From the saucy little liar

Two Black Feathers

From where I do not know
Two black Ravens came along
Or even why to me they came
This place they don't belong

Two black Ravens did implore
Came peering through my door
Their soulless eyes welcomed me
A sight I should ignore

Their feathers wore a darkness
Colder than the night
They swallowed up the light
And chilled my bones alright

And move along the floor they did
Nor a sound or reason why
The blackness in them Ravens
Just made me want to die

A Black Raven

A raven came in triumph
In silence from the blackest night
Crisp autumn leaves fell as shadows
Lay burnt limp and lifeless

The brittle iron of winters grasp
Blew coldly in its clasp
Then struck down a gauntly bird
Who never said never a word?

The musical notes came from hell
Stood tall and played farewell
Until all that remains is silence
And a Raven in the fall

 LARRY DICKENS

Cracked

The sound of silence cracked
Icy frost as sharp as needles
Clung to him like lead
Neither should abandon him

Outside the snow rolled in cold amber light
Strangers quietly sit with drawn faces
In old forbidden places
brittle trees hang lifelessly to gunmetal skies

Memories become hollow and forgotten
His future yours truly holds despair
As cold snaps at his claws and splitting feathers
Not even the devil may-care

Parched' no longer seeking warmth
with eyes as black as onyx
His mind bent on injustice
Forbids all thoughts of bliss

Until a shattering broken silence
Cracks open every nervous look
From those whose lives are spent
Comes a cold lonely rook

Doors

The light enters as the darkness leaves
Closing the door shut as it grieves
A pointless future playing-the-game
Where no-one else takes the blame

Looking long into a two-way mirror
There's no way in and no way back
Just a shadowy life of debt and doubt
With joyless feelings there's no way out

Revolving doors like passing trains
Caught people in the dashing rain
Running to the underground
Downstairs to the lost and found

A journey to a world unknown
To places some souls call home
A one-way ticket and looking ahead
A summoning from the restless dead

The distant past left behind
A shallow life of hollowed dreams
Across the bridge a final ride
To catch our train to the other side

   LARRY DICKENS

Genesis

Sunday morning moss gently lifts the
Snowdrops nestled amongst dancing
Shadows of the sylvan glade
Beyond there, slate rock splinters
With evergreen shrubs
Bordering the peninsula

The sunrise chases' cotton clouds
That gather like horses galloping
With vines stretching to
Touch bristling moss as it clings to the last
Dew before sunlight snatches it away

A fluttering amongst the trees disturbs
The silence of the glade as sweetly as
A harp might dance to fingers as soft as
Summer rain pattering the forest floor

The dawn vapour swirled
Above the shimmering lake
Reflecting its timeless existence as
Life within the forest played
Out the breaking of the day

Woodlarks sing to the heavens
Transforming the forest with the ever
Expectance of newness and vigour to
Taste the blended riches of Gods
Creation as its always meant to be

A Life Worthwhile

You make my life worthwhile
With your perfect smile
Each day my heart belongs to you
In treasured keeping made anew
I love the freshness of your scent
Its sweeter than the morning dew
I love your eyes of heavenly blue
When they see me watching you?

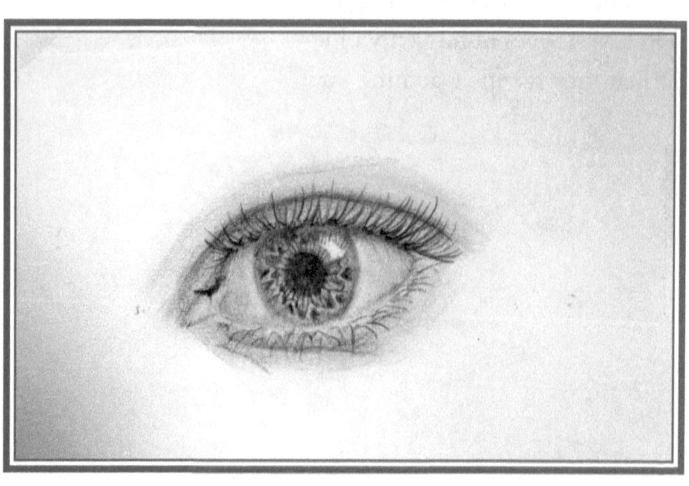

The Lonely Wind

Somewhere on a cold night
A wind lonely blew
To a dark bleak November
Under winters watchful gaze

The child wind sought shelter
Hustling with rustling Autumn leaves
Blowing to places long forgotten
Now abandoned and begotten

Down hollowed out trees it blew
Along baron deserted beaches
Through sculpted dunes in decay
It blew until the break of day

April

My dear, such richness for us
Turning a corner into spring
Brilliant sunshine with Kites on the wing
Green fields shoring up yon valley
Wood ants scuttling over felt moss
Red Admirals basking on slatted stone
And Wrens seen darting
Beneath lazy bracken
Emerging victorious to song as sweet as you
A welcome breeze a coolness
Just as you please
As we picnic amongst the trees

At the Beach

Champagne sea for miles, awash with deep blues
Gently rolling to pebbled shores, the colour of caramel
Single people, couples and families dotted along the coastline
All facing the sea under a July sun
Cotton clouds paint clear blue skies
Forming shapes with gentle sighs
A postcard picture of prevalence
As people once more taste the salty sea air
The champagne sun flows and sways
With the beaches and sea of Branscomb Bay

Broken

Drifting but I let it go unspoken
long before I stopped
I had broken, you had never said a word
Letting it all go to a sullen unheard
Your sexy scent never left me
Lingering sweetly embracing me and weeping
In your rapture your touch so long ago
Felt strikingly new as did the tingling that famed on my lips
Those false dawns wrapping me in
Pushing me further to the edge of reason
But you held me close, so close it hurt
Giving me your heart your love your life
Undone I never told you how far I drifted to places
You could not find me eventually darkness came
And I lost you, morning brought stillness and no you
Months wandering left me searching
Breaching the walls of my heart to breaking
Never knowing such love unrelenting
If you missed me loved me or not at all

     LARRY DICKENS

Carousel

You take my breathe with words that caress my skin
I close my eyes and my dreams invite you in
I send you a rose whose petals unfold the colour of your blush
My heart beats loud do you hear the sound… hush

Too much too soon, flying high with the moon
As I lay my head on your featherlight bed
With your words of love echoing in my head

For once more a love I meet
Makes me whole and feel complete
Sharing secrets and telling no lies
Just longing to hold you and look into your eyes.

You are to me such a beautiful love
Out of nowhere from God above
An angel a sun-soaked kiss
My carousel of heavenly bliss

Covidia

Roads as grey as metallic skies endlessly twisting and turning
Lay silent and baron scarring the landscape in a world that
    ground to a halt
The grass verges once neatly lined give way to weeds that
    do impress
Reclaiming territory long lost to human progress

It may as well be night, yet the clock strikes midday in the
    month of May
Time had moved with the sun and moon
While everything else stood still
Such was the air tasteless and filled with doom

The virus laid waste with so much haste
A disease called confusion and Covidia was born
It changed the world that stopped in its tracks
As it marched against the scientist facts

Public houses remained boarded up as deserted streets
    looked on
Homes became prisons its residents peering through
    drawn curtains
Playgrounds once packed with children
Lie empty chilling the air with deathly silence

The world moved inside their homes glued to digital platforms
2 meters apart became the norm, as close as it got
Facebook was finally pulling its weight, even as Zoom
    came in late
Twitter feeds shrilled with Trumped up news
As Instagram held a million stills

Outside was handed back to mother nature call
Singing its victory chorus with each new dawn
The old got sick, too many gave way
The young got busy clicking and typing each day

People became digital heroes like Major Tom
Walking 99 laps and some
Each step worth more than the awards he got
Not long after many forgot

Silence engulfed the wise for once
Their words had no meaning carrying no weight
The young had a revolution supressing their oppression
With laptops and keyboards unable to date

People feared even their own, ordering food on their phone
Some shuffled like lambs to supermarkets
Making toilet rolls their main target
While others to old remained at home silent and all alone

Mothers gritted their teeth rising above
As children stared unable to love
Some fathers some husbands some men called time
Long after the wine had left

It should have been raining with clouds as dark as night
Obliterating the heavens of all its light
The air should have been stifling and heavy
As an old man passed with a stick unsteady

The sun shone across the nation
As clouds stayed on vacation
In short, a glorious spring that undid
Mother nature smiled and humanity hid

It added to strange times echoed by many standing in line
No sound of airplanes over head
Just faceless people like the walking dead
Waiting with hearts filled with dread

Some said it's the end times
Others still called it judgement
Apologetics came up with excuses
As idealist became recluses

The world just stopped everything else just carried on
It wasn't meant to be this way, humanity had lost its grip
As the unseen enemy took hold
Laying waste to the sick and the old

Progress was brought to its knees
Others declared peace at last, as the ruling class stumbled
    in the dark
As one world disappeared none could undo
A digital world exploded clear into view

Then came the clapping
Those valiant nightingales of the NHS
Whose working hours did impress
Almost as much as the carers with less

Politicians stood up and praised their work
Rallying to their side, unable to hide
But none spoke of the dead
As churches stopped breaking the bread

Plans got ripped up, shredded in digital waste
People changed habits in earnest and haste
Drifting with the crowds on-line
Instead of running with wolves outside

Street crime stopped like trains out of track
Increasing its activities on the information highways
Now everyone's running with the pack
Afraid to ever look back

Stay home stay safe protect the NHS
Be alert remember the rule of six
2 meters apart with a shopping cart
Hands face space don't look out of place

Safety inched further away for the abused
Theirs was a hidden virus for the accused
Festering beneath wounds of deceit
Laying waste to every woman and child they meet

Ships became Petri dishes and some abandoned
Their captives unaware the crew went overboard
T.V. crews smiled giving hope to millions
Unable to hold on to the same old newsreel

The furloughed languished as time elapsed
While the self-employed withered and collapsed
Politicians kept checking their diary
For handling a public enquiry

People got cycling in Lycra clad shorts
Some working from home many alone
Pools were closed and no more sports
The like of which had never been known

And time ensnared us all again
Even those standing out in the rain
We carry on regardless
Unable to laugh or simply complain

Covidia found its way into the hearts of men
New words for the dictionary but no-one knows when
Soon climate change took over the news
And Covidia became the norm we could not undo

Dead End

Eyes watching the pavement looking down unable to view
  the sky
Shame brought on the guilt of trips to shops with over
  stacked trollies
People work alone amidst the chaos of nurses working
  double shifts
To save the lives of those whose lives are already spent

The news reels roll on like sirens in the dark corners of
  every home
Bringing more despair of yet another humanitarian disaster
Journalist asking a question in a dozen different tones
The only answer comes is more isolation and everyone alone

The dog roams the streets unable to decide which way to go
No longer hindered by the lights of cars or drunken screams
The old man looks out onto the street and no longer sees
  the world
In a box he stands quietly waiting for his time

The rarest of sounds comes from the radio shack
Echoes of further deaths that could not be helped
The doctors ran out of ventilators the nurses out of the ICU
Wisdom had departed and the children gave up too

Everyone has an opinion and some more than most
No one listens, people turn over in bed
Time has become faint and for some it is lost
On all but the living amongst the dead

Everyday

Thinking of you, and every day since
No longer here, you found sense and left
Snowdrifts clamber against the back door
Because no-one leaves, you come no-more

All the things we promised and said
Recalling holding hands in bed
Tightly knit in case you fled
Or if you'd had enough instead

Storm clouds gather like crimson shrouds
Blanketing skies their suffering colour
That fades away just as I do
When searching out for you

I forget how much I love you
When you were once all mine
Or how I'd kissed your lips
And tasted your sweet wine
Or when together we reached the skies
Before you left and said goodbyes

    LARRY DICKENS

My heart broken held to the crestfallen moon
Seeking the stars that would become you
The heavens watched with bated breath
To see such love, die all too soon

Now all that remains are words that flow
Over stepping stones and brittle old bones
As if a lifetime slips quietly away
Forgetting the memories made long ago

The Rain.

Falling upon the heavy-laden floors
Laying waste to blind faith
Soldiers marched into bloodied streets
Far from peace in places evergreen

Somewhere in the distance a swing sways to a cold wind
Its chains rasping with the pain of rusty metal
A cat edges deeper into the undergrowth
with eyes long lost to sleep

The fanatic screams out his Discordia
With hatred he pushes the trip switch
The last thing he ever does
The God of peace is finally at war

With the ungodliness and the apathetic
The chaos of the religious rabbi
Whose teaching are written in blood

Throughout the night
Came the sky in gunmetal grey
The rain followed
Crestfallen like a moon that cannot reach the stars

The light pierced the darkness
The sight of man brought mourning
Like a passing train in the distance
It cannot be affected
For it will be long gone at dawn

The Souls' Lay Down

Man, the hero for the love
Brave in the battle
Courage over adversity
Wielding power of life over death
A soldier of a thousand hearts

Man, the grief of him
The souls that lay beside his feet
Gather as shadows in the dust
Long lost to a war with no wages
And death yet forsakes the hero

Alone beside the girl he fought for
And now unable to teach himself
He understands only the waste
Of the nameless one without

After a thousand deaths yearn
A heart to see the sea
A soul to lay down beside the road
And sleep that crushes the distant
Memories that bled red on the battlefield
Long into the darkest night...

Nephilim Prayer

You are as Nephilim to me
As ash to the fiery mountain
Does this set me apart?
Then it is my beating heart

There, you stand as tall as Rephaites
Whilst I toil for your currency
That gathers like sin to your door
Even as I gather the bread crumbs from your fleshing floor

Yet my heart is not yours
Nor my soul, or my thoughts
For they belong to Adonai; Lord of Creation
Set apart like yeast at the Passover

So, take your riches and glorify your deeds
For your inheritance is earthly bound
But I will wait for the Kingdom of Heaven
In sufferance with a joyful heart

 LARRY DICKENS

Every inclination of my soul bends to sin
Like the grass in the prairie winds
I will not break
My feet are like its roots
Holding firm to the good soil

You take that is the effort of the labourer
And pay for the wages of sin
I'll wash myself in the blood of Christ
And pay my dues to God.

The Cheviots Sky

The rolling Cheviots with its gorged valleys
Are like high seas on the horizon
Drifting as explorers might
To places of great adventures seen

The hills plateaued and plunged
Their weary graceful ways
Rising up to heavens'
And falling to green fields below

It could have been a summers day
But for the icy arctic winds
Open skies and cotton clouds
Looked upon black faced sheep fluffed up

The lonely heights and meandering valleys
Flowed in pursuit of winters heather
Nestling against the mossy slate
Where clumps of snowdrops lay in wait

Each hill and slope decorated another
Giving its beauty to every skyline
Every summit drew closer to heaven
Honouring its reverence of God

     LARRY DICKENS

<h1 style="text-align:center">Passing by</h1>

Do you walk with the wind?
In your sails cheerfully bright
Or do you run wild
In the dales fearfully white

When you look into clear blue skies
And tell yourself to forget-me-knot
Does your shadow also follow?
Your beauty or perhaps not

When the leaves gather at your feet
As you amble along the forest floor
Do you kick them side to side?
Or welcome them even more

When the song thrush sings to you
Do you sing along too?
Or do you listen with a joyful heart
In case the moment should thence depart

And when you pray to the Lord your God
Do you cup your hands and confess?
Or raise your arms to heavens
As you plead His forgiveness

When the embers within the fireplace
Are lost to your tearful eyes
Do you wander down memory lane?
And whisper your soft goodbyes

　　　LARRY DICKENS

Lost

And you built your love quietly
Giving lessons I could not learn
With love you pulled it down
Leaving nothing but the remains
Of another winters day

That same ambiguous smile
The little frown that appears with
Eyes that hold my gaze
Until I see the evident denial
Of a kiss you cannot give

Too many bridges too much water
And not enough time together
The silly things we fought for
The importance of every day
Fading beyond our dreams

Weaving that tapestry of trust
That turned to friendship
That lasted beyond your years
Your outflow of emotional brokenness
Still brings my tears
Long after the dust of us

Love is...

You are beautiful inside and out
Like the rain that patters on a hot summers' night
Or the wood smoke drifting along the meadows
You are the snow in the winter as you sit in front of your
    home fire
Reading a book in your favourite arm chair
You are the taste of melting toast
The smell of freshly cut grass
The bread in the oven and coffee in the pot
You are the words that escape me
The joy that fills me
You are the seasons wrapped up in me all at once
You are the birds chirping happily in the morning dew
You are the touch that wakes me up with a smile
The kiss that never leaves me
You are all this and more
You are my heart beat
My love, my every thought
Love has never been so beautiful
As the days I spend with you

LARRY DICKENS

In-between

Out of nothing
A rapture that cannot be seen
A sound that cannot be heard
A vision too bright to understand

Your touch, silk and satin as soft as the petals upon a rose
Your voice like music dances between the folds of my heartbeat
Your smile as beautiful as meadows in midsummer
Your beauty intoxicating becomes my breathless desire

Where every dream comes true
Amongst the flowers and morning dew
No flaws or lines to fall between
Each time I look at you

That laughter braver than the moon
Cares not for the darkness
Shines brighter all the more
With the one I do adore

Warm affectionate and infectious
Longing to breathe the air you breath
A second becomes eternity with you
A day without leave

Finding you compares thee to a butterfly
A moth to flames
The first shoots of spring
The beginning the end and all the in-betweens

Held together like a tapestry
Yearning to be free
The moment you see me
Unable to leave or say goodbye

The spark that ignites the old wood
Becomes a flame becoming an unbridled inferno
Lost to you with breathless desire
We burn together until we are ashes and no more

And the dust of us becomes as ethereal
Like the way you once touched me
As fragile and light as snow
Now drifts in time dancing with the stars

No longer no more and everything
Something and nothing
Memories held together in a fire
Beyond the light and darkness

Does your kiss not linger long after?
Even your words whisper to me at night
Your touch tingles and dances on my skin
Even your eyes watching me within

Your smile still joyfully echoes
As we fly freely away in spaces between
Memories held together with delicate strands
Separated from everything else

Like they don't belong and yet, have always
For they are all that's left of you
And all that's left of me
Are the things that set us free

War

Losing sight of all the things you once cared so much for
Then trying to figure out why you cared at all
Nothing matters it happens behind closed doors
We trip out and stumble and fall

The arguments keep pressing on like waves rattling against
    decaying cliffs
The louder they get the louder we scream
Until the no one hears anything at all
And then comes the silence

The simple things become impassable
The complicated things get left on the shelf
Apathy is cloaking you like a comfort blanket
Disguised only by the colours that run

Love drained from already empty souls
Standing still with nowhere to go
Flowers once graced in rainbow colours
Now lifeless as dark as coals

Their kind once despised now our kind
As it all looks the same
Politicians losing their mind
Long after playing the blame game

Climate change forgotten in rage
As forest greens went up in flames
History ran out of pages
The world was never the same

War upon war in these evil times
Echoes of apathy's aftermath
To late too little and too much wine
Humanity succumbed to its own wrath

     LARRY DICKENS

Saviour

Christ my Lord remembered me
The stones beneath my naked feet
Any thoughts of hurt lay beneath
Cry out to God to rescue me
To wash away my sins to sea

Christ my Lord remembered me
The chains he broke with my plea
With His blood he shed for me
And paid the price to set me free

Each breath I take with his grace
Guided to a heavenly place
The Holy Spirit within my soul
Helps me reach my goal

Nothing too much or too hard
With you my Lord at my side
It is my heart that you guard
For it is in me you do abide

As I lay down at your feet
Rescued from the stones beneath
I cry to you my loving Lord
For it was you who remembered me

Spectral

The only friends I have
belong to me and only me
Called loneliness and silence
They both abandon me
Just when I need them most
Like I'm the cause of all their woe
Wherever I seem to go

I'm unoriginal in most respects
That's why I live alone
Nothing fancy to see
You wouldn't want to be me
Nothing to offer or even a home
With just the streets to roam

Being old is like a blessing
No longer down the pub
or eating rubbish grub
Once no time to cook
Or time to think of you
There always seemed too much to do
With not a single clue

    LARRY DICKENS

Now time seems to linger
And wants to be my friend
But just like the other two
Drives me round the bend
But when I need it most
It's like a spectral ghost
And leaves me Just like you

Apathy

As it goes the days are like rain
Words drip from the newsstand laced with empty rhetoric
The world is at a tribunal no-one notices
decay creeps within every generation

Humanity has come to its fleshing floor
None could be spared
A fall from grace as spectacular as it is sad
The Lord of murder rises in the East

Found to have a name for righteousness
Within every broken heart
For sin knows no boundaries
Forever seeking its own resume

At birth the heart cried out in sorrow at the night
The longing for death had begun in earnest
There came comfort in the mourning
And sadness at the table of rich delight

A wretched soul already knows its destiny
Death has found its place
Amongst the living and the dead
Even those whose hearts had bled

    LARRY DICKENS

Rain Swept Love

Rain falling across windswept moors
And then you smile
You give me all your love
And swept it away
Reaching out
holding onto the sun
Before it falls from view
Your delicious face
Lighting up hearts in every place
Causes me too sing
Racing with clouds
On breathless wings
Looking at you now
In the cold light of day
Nothing can compare
The night we shared
The morning after
Having spent everything

Snowdrops on Annfield Plains

Snowdrops falling on Annfield Plain
Drifting across to the moors
I see you too
A heart shaped star

Your eyes smiling at the swirling flakes
And tears as crystal as diamonds sparkle
Your dreams carried away in the moment
And melting away hearts in every moorland flower

I see you falling like the snow
Each kiss remembered
Under the light of the falling sun
And I want to fall with you

Your arms spread out and soaring
The angels watch adoring
Caught in the snow
No man can follow

As you fall and drift up in the skies
And catch the flakes of melting hearts
I find myself falling once again
Falling in love with you

  LARRY DICKENS

 Night Life

The faint hum of a distant horn out to sea gathers pace
Some call it tinnitus where others may call it a sound of place
Failing the paracetamol is like walking in the rain
	forgetting an overcoat
Yet this is peace compared to the cramps, so please take note

Sleep comes as easily as the night falls
And leaves before the midnight hour as taut cramps call
Shoulders hunched and muscles taut as iron

Sitting alone downstairs with eyes cold watching the
	seconds roll into minutes
Soon to become hours as dawn creeps up against the walls
Unable to deter the damn pain the wretched body complains
As bloodshot eyes no longer care grow weary and fall

The distant fog horns once relentless charge, give way to
	morning dew
Sounding no more as if the need no longer mattered
Stretched muscles relaxed once more sigh against the shadows
As paracetamol finally takes over and eases into dawn

Sleep comes once more again after the night-life
Having nothing more to say with the coming of a new day
The digital alarm rings from outside long needed dreams
Cursing the eyes to open abandonment

Another day and another life
Relief is but short and shrift
Only a matter of time and just a moment of peace
Until we go again adrift in a sea of pain

 LARRY DICKENS

Leave me to my losses

The sound you hear is inside us
Echoes of every word we spoke
Ring out as clear as day
We looked to see if Christ is with us

There are times when I am on bended knee
The emptiness is greater than the fullness of my heart
The measure breaks up the sounds as they come to me
Too much hurt, leave me to my losses

Pity overwhelms me
The sounds of people underwhelming
They have nothing to say
Let me go, just leave me to my losses

Did you know me, did you see me?
As the crow flies did you follow me
Such a short walk to find me
But you remained a statue

Running into a chasm of despair you never followed
Thank heavens for its no place to be
When darkness is all, you see
Let me go, just leave me to me losses

And did you know
That the skies bowed with majestic thunder
Right after the lightning strikes
Shattering the peace into submission

I came across you next to me
Is this the place we find ourselves?
The simple things that we once were have left us
So, leave me to my losses

We could once rely upon each other
To feel safe in each other
But then we ask ourselves
Let me go, leave me to my losses

The music play in the distance
Critical acclaim bouncing off the walls
Its sound reverberating inside my heart
Let me go, leave me to my losses

   LARRY DICKENS

Pimley Bridge

They built that highway
Across those rugged pastures
Where a stone bridge lays
Not far from some rickety woods

About the bridge thrived such wonders
Water Boatmen, Dragonfly and more
Like lanky Bulrushes, lazy Lilies
Damselflies and noisy little Natterjacks

The pond itself sprung from the brook
Their borders snaffled by bracken
Further beyond with a careful eye
You'd venture Kingfishers or even A Rook

Willows and Hazels swayed in the breeze
Nestling between wild red roses seen
Ragwort and Nettles lay siege ahead
To a path no longer tread

The bridge itself stood Haunting
Holding memories that of a child
in fair and gentler times, you'd say
When children then did play

To glorious summers days
With the sun climbing to the blue
And melting away springs dew
To. Echo's only children knew...

"This is our side, on guard'!' And this Is ours, stand back"
In the meadow fields, girls giggled...
Singing "he loves me, he loves me not"
While threading daisy chains too

"Charge• cried someone!
Amidst Such joyous rapture of laughter
That's the way it used to be in those endless summers
When motes danced in the sunlight
Of Pimley Bridge and a boy

Vampires

And bitterness filled her beauty
Lith was her rapture
Ash clouds stole her skies
Bleeding men's cries

A symphony wrought a harrowing
In the chaos of her blackened silk
Until all that's left is death
And death had followed her ilk

She took the goblet that he was
Tearing down through his flesh
And darkness came from hell
With screams unheard he fell

And beauty drank her prey
With bloodied lips and eyes of grey
T'was this her wine and bread
Of souls that laydown dead

And darkly did he look
Her dominion sealed his fate
He took upon her form
Laying low deep did he wait

    LARRY DICKENS

Long shadows echoed terror
Their passing like a curse
Came falling on their victims
Soon followed by a hearse

His chiselled features drawn
To the sunken depths of her
Caste love and hate together
And bloodlust borne forever

Mile End Meadow

Kissing softly amidst the Snowdrops
Braced against winters breath
The taste of your lips like wine
Lingers sweetly as your perfume
Long after the protracted goodbye

Knowing we had lost all we were
Breathless in the weariness we shared
I loved the very bones of you
And the dust they were soon to become
And the dust of you like Motes in the moonlight
Would rise up in the air floating across the Glebe

In its wake love followed whispering your name
Against the backdrop of Snowdrops
And Saint Augustine Meadows

 LARRY DICKENS

Sorrow

An age has passed
Snow came then left
Like you

Spring unfurled her arms
Into summer
And still no you

Drifting aimlessly
Haunting those old places
We no longer shared

Memories revisited when in
Summers dream you came into being
Like exothermic lightning

I miss the sight of you now
And the sight of you I loved
Never leaving

You completed me then
In life now death
And sorrow

The Reaping

Church bells chapels morgues
Carriages black at dawn
Faces lost like silent ghosts
Near dusty old tombstones

The sun has finely set
No longer in its debt
Long shadows softly drawn
Felt old grey and worn

The reaper came a reaping
Mourners came a weeping
Praying at the pews
On knees I paid my dues

And paid in full I had
Of that I'm faintly glad
I'd made the purple patch
Before he did dispatch

No tussles for deserving or saying
It's too severe on knees praying
My debt to him is paid
At reaping did I fade

Sleep Paralysis

There are no loose boards
If there were, they'd be creaking?
Lying under a crest fallen moon
In silence and pending doom

The pool is shimmering black
As cool as midnight sky
Came humming a lullaby
Take a look why don't you spy

Looking down to spirited faces
Long lost without a trace
Feral screams from behind
Long lost to their kind

From my blindside
Her haunting she did hide
The floorboards they did creak
From my mind I did leap

Springing through the dark
My knees pulled to my heart
I leapt to the unknown
And heard myself groan

 LARRY DICKENS

This is the way it always begins
Whispering "it's safe, fall in"
Fall into the shimmering black
Knowing there's no way back

I'm drowning in those faces
The withering of the place
Those bloodshot eyes were calling
In icy waters, falling

Further from salvation
Flailing in the blackness
Pins and needles jagged knives
The dead become alive

Stricken fearful turning back
My hopes were all but hung
From where I'd leapt and hung
Stood the darkest soulless hack

In pitch of night and cloaked in death
No eyes or mouth or winters breath
A darkling there she stood
A crimson hell misunderstood

Breathless for her to see
Such blackness did she weep
Graven faces welcomed me
Afterall its only sleep

I was but a sojourner
Chilled with mortal fear
I heard her ghastly murmur
The last thing I did hear

　　　　　LARRY DICKENS

Vacant

Derelict that's the heart
Hollowed out deserted
Abandoned left to rot
Vacant in the lot

Broken brittle crumbling sway
Shattered glass gone astray
Cracked and crooked they'll see
That's me no longer free

The eyes faded jaded grey
The lips cracked in dismay
Hair as heavy as lead
Vacant almost dead

The Lord and Job 1

The ashen clouds parted
Bringing forth the light of the heavens
And the Lord spoke
All four corners of the earth trembled
From the foundations to where the cornerstones assembled
At His word the darkness broke
And there was day and
The morning starts rose out of the night sky singing too
    the angels
Dressed in rivers of joy and
The proud sea rose to the morning sun
With graceful waves until undone
The Lord laid garments over the oceans
Lace clouds and rainbows shawls
That stretched from shore to shore
And gave the dawn aroma
A place to call its own

     LARRY DICKENS

The Lord and Job 3

May the day of my birth never begin
That hapless night conceived a boy shackled to sin
I pray to the God of heaven
Look away! Forget this night
For darkness surrounds me
Where light does not belong

Depression lays waste my soul
The joy of God departing me
To brokenness and debt
My oceans of deepest fear
Too numerous to be counted
To real to be untrue leave me without
For emptiness cannot be filled ignored or routed

Though the morning stars are known by name
They too wait in vain
For the light of dawn to come again

A boy I was born
To a mother unable to abandon me
Or hide the disappointment on her face
As she left me without a trace

It would have been better I was stillborn
Then a crown of thorns
It would have been better I rested
In a coffin beneath the ground
Then find myself a slave
With mortal sin abound

This misery of my soul
Seeks no treasure life can offer
For it has been hidden from me
Till death that sets me free

My bitterness weeps as tears
Falling at my door
To God oh God I do implore
No more I beg of thee
Take my wretched soul
Break my heart and set me free

Stanhope Moors

The heather strewn moors are
Dressed as for a wedding gift
Shaded browns mingling in the soft moss
Whose greens and yellows glisten in the amber morning sun
A chilly wind ebbs and sways through the moorland
Its touch a reminder of where we're at
Stone walls reflect the colour of cumulous clouds
As ashen as the splintered slate
Each stone equal in size too large to move
Stand as pillars defying the makers strength
The expanse above bathed in
Royal blues as puffed up storm clouds loom
Go on forever and ever more they go
Its majesty to awesome to describe hangs as a picture
Painting blue heavens above
Black faced sheep meander lazily through the heather
Seemingly oblivious to the freshness of this place
Followed by lambs with coats as gentle as drifting snow
Not a sound, just a tender wind kissing the landscape
As it rises to the heavens above
With silence it breathes its loving kiss
Both heaven and earth as one
The horizon rises and dips
Holding up gunmetal skies, stretching towards the sun
    moon and stars
This place of tranquillity where God speaks
Is heavenly when seen with open eyes and a receiving heart
A blessing for all those who care to see

You Are

You are the amber sun as it rises from the East
You are the autumn colours
Before they undress for the winter snow
You are the morning freshness that breaks free from the night

Your perfume is a thousand flowers
That undress the courts of kings and queens
You are the shadow on the ground
That never leaves me in the lost and found

You are as sweet as freshly cut grass
On a spring morning after the dew
You are the woodsmoke in the forest
That smoulders like your eyes

You are the splendour in the leaves
As they tumble from the trees
You are the rain on a hot summers' day
Washing over us wherever we lay

 LARRY DICKENS

Suddenly

Young children out playing
And suddenly…

Red tiled roofs and overcast skies
Suddenly
Young children running church bells ringing
Then suddenly
A small face a scented flower
Suddenly sweet
Fluttering overhead, rain splashed paths
A sudden dash
A boy whoops
The bride stoops
A sudden gasp
Such a pretty face
With some floral grace
All of a sudden

Springtime in the Trossachs

Pretty petite bonnets
Sit proudly upon the mountains
A sparkling sunrise champagnes
Lifts daffodils from their slumber

A verdurous evergreen forest gives way
To open fields dressed in snow
And beyond across the mist
An ebony lake shimmers in the breeze

Many a pilgrim came too late
Missing the seduction of the place
Its mysteries at dawn lost
Long after the morning dew

Haughmond Hill

This place so bold
Why am I here
Searching out the boy
Or to watch the sky unfold

My memories of old
Stood in a chilled breeze
A place of my soul
So complete and whole
With its secrets and feral ways

To stop and take in breath
Gulp down the ages
Of memories long held
And echoes of joy
When I was but a boy

My soul longed to this place
Its tranquillity and peace
As I nestled in her bosom
For she is deep in the heart of me

The Rest

Come rest a while
Lay down your weary way
Be true to all you hold dear
Be still
For I am near
Rest in my arms and breath
Take in the beauty of my nature
For it is given freely
For those who take time to see

Her Love

She like rain poured tears
Filling her heart with broken promises
Left collecting dust as
A book put down
Misplaced and now unfound
Remembered words with torn pages

Too long unspoken
In letters given with hearts on sleeves
Amidst stolen kisses of a lover's dream
He cast his place with the cold East wind
Now blown to places new

Recalling a romance with delicate petals
Swept away by the ebbing tide
Of memories shared with no place to hide
Amidst the broken hearts and morning cries

You Silly

She joked about me
Speaking out of turn
Avoiding me her kindness
A lesson hard to learn

She never told me why
Nothing but a lie
Soon after she left me
Not even a goodbye

I've never let her go
So, she cut herself free
Then quietly let me know
It's you silly, not me

I Love You

Jewelled sands beneath drifting
As my floating thoughts run adrift
To the harmony of looping waves
And sprawling skies of blue
I consider no one but you

Your lightest touch to a whisper
My heart to yours I confide
With the sands of our time
Just rolling gently aside
Then falling softly back

No trace of footfalls
That we once passed by
Just the quiet lingering presence
Of a lover's lullaby

Under blue falling skies
And delicate folds of watery petals
We kissed upon blushing shores
Before returning to our deepest sleep
And treasured dreams for us to keep.

Moonlight Love

The last of the black ashen clouds give way to the edge of
    the world
Leaving behind a landscape so solemnly serene
A quiet place, a picture still, not a sound, hush
As the light ebbs and falls away, a sacred moon holds sway
My heart the colour of blood trembled in its dusty light
It was the afterglow
The glow given after making love
She like Lodestone pulled me in
I like iron filings drawn to her
Through the air that held the tranquil scent of fir trees
Meadow grass and aging bark of grand old oak trees
And with its ambiance, the very air seems to have an oldness
Breathing life into its surroundings
And as I was drawn to her
So was the aging scent of love drawn to us
And we breathed in our love
Under a harvest moon we made our love
Like a soft rain the world returned to us
With it her sounds and shadows
The shadows fell like leaves around our naked forms
And danced within the flames of our passions
Autumn drew her breath
And our souls rejoiced
As she like love drew breath
And in love exhaled

   LARRY DICKENS

A Lonely Wind

Somewhere on a cold night
A wind lonely blew
To a dark bleak November
Under winters watched gaze

The child wind sought shelter
Hustling with rustling autumn leaves
Blowing to places long forgotten
Now abandoned and begotten

Down hollowed out trees it blew
Along baron deserted beaches
Through sculptured dunes in decay
It blew until the break of day

Old Grey Smoke

Smoke gets in your eyes
Manufacturers tell you lies
To which your mind defies
Cancer comes to no surprise
And still all hope denies
Even after we say goodbye

Families watch as your life sighs
Every sinew within subsides
Until the moment love dies
Broken hearts and mourning cries
Surround your coffin in black ties
All your questions get no replies
As old grey smoke gets in your eyes

Isolation

Isolations' becoming a legacy
Forecasting breathless emptiness
Stories in pictures remain untold
Framed by a concealed prophecy

The same song repeats, plays
Its restless lullaby in apathy
Filling the spaces in a vacant room
Until the sound drowns out all the days

Routines drift in from the past
Into a future already seen
And the lifelines becoming contexed
Until the first becomes the last

Long Gone

I drift like an abandoned ship
An empty vessel looking outwards to nether
I'm thinking of you and broken,
And it sounds like…
Snapped twigs in the dark
And it feels like
I'm floundering like a whale
In a goldfish bowel
I count the aged lines
Upon my beaten weathered face
A map of all my journeys
And realise
I've lost my youth
For it has long gone
Just like you

  LARRY DICKENS

Forgotten

At dawn the skylark sings
A raven lifts its wings to the sun
Adjustment in earnest has begun

Forgotten poetry on dusty shelves
Now taken down and read by bed
With a heart as heavy as lead

Outside a crimson burnt out sky
A bitter wind blows through the day
Long after children went out to play

Bedtime stories no longer told
A lullaby no longer sung
And kisses like birds have flown

Now lost in dreams once held
A ring with nowhere to go
Its weight once light as snow

Quietness surrounds each room
As time gently slips away
Away until the end of day

Hurtful Things

My thoughts spill over
Longing as it is
I miss you
Feeling I needed to
My self-preservation forgotten
To a conflict long begotten
I thought I knew you
Then came the double take
Up all night coldly awake
Thoughts swimming upstream
Every part of me screaming
It's plain you're emotionally through
With that you tell me too
Those tears run dry
Leaving drawn out sighs
Questions asking why?
Such hurtful things
We wretched souls
We love we lose we hate
And fill our hearts with sorrow

If I were to love anyone
It would be you I love
The considered heart considers no more
All my thoughts Lying at your door
If I was to march into war
I would march with you beside me
For your beauty would fell a thousand men
Who would fall to you on bended knee?
If I were to love anyone it would be you
For to you my heart stays true.

Silent Love

Not a word spoken
Nor breath taken in vain
Or an inconsiderate truth
We find ourselves once again
Alone with broken dreams
We pass each other
As if not there
Strangers now become us
Not a word or sound
A look of care
We find ourselves once again
Alone with broken dreams
If I touch the ground
And feel the earth under my weight
And look see beyond
I may yet know my place
And be filled with grace
Then with an open heart
I would listen to your dream
In silences heard
Those memories filled
That once was us
When we were not lost in silence
Our dreams once more alive

 LARRY DICKENS

Fiery Love

I wanted so much to wake in the morning at your side
I can't explain the troubles we hide
If you were to return to me
It would be to you my heart would confide

I could not find the strength in my heart
After all the things we have been through
You have shown me love and how hard it is to depart
You brought me sunshine in beautiful skies blue
You have my soul completely into you

When you are in my life it is an endless summer
Without you it is a bitter cold winter
When we first met, I knew it was true
Because my life had just started because of you

I am giving all my love from the bottom of my heart
I beg of us not to rip it all apart
The things we do and the things we say
Wishing our love far away
My heart like yours pounding at the door
The shattered remains on a broken floor.